W9-BES-120

Timeline of Columbus's Life

1451

Christopher Columbus is born in Genoa, Italy, to a family of wool workers.

1480–1490

Columbus plans a westward voyage to the Spice Islands of Asia.

1476–1477

Columbus sails to England and Ireland. He studies history, geography, astronomy, and navigation.

1461

Columbus goes to sea for the first time, at age ten.

1482–1485

Columbus makes trading voyages along the west coast of Africa.

1479

While working in Portugal, Columbus marries a Portuguese noblewoman.

1492–1493

Sponsored by the king and queen of Spain, Columbus crosses the Atlantic Ocean, believing he has reached Asia. He becomes governor of all the lands he claims for Spain.

1502–1504

Columbus goes on his fourth voyage, to the Caribbean and Central America. He is shipwrecked on Jamaica for a year, then rescued.

1493–1496

Columbus goes on his second voyage, to the Caribbean.

1498–1500

Columbus goes on his third voyage, to the Caribbean and South America. He quarrels with Spanish officials and mistreats native peoples. He is dismissed as governor and sent back to Spain as a prisoner.

1506

Ill and exhausted, Columbus dies in Spain, still believing that he had reached Asia.

Map of Columbus's Voyages

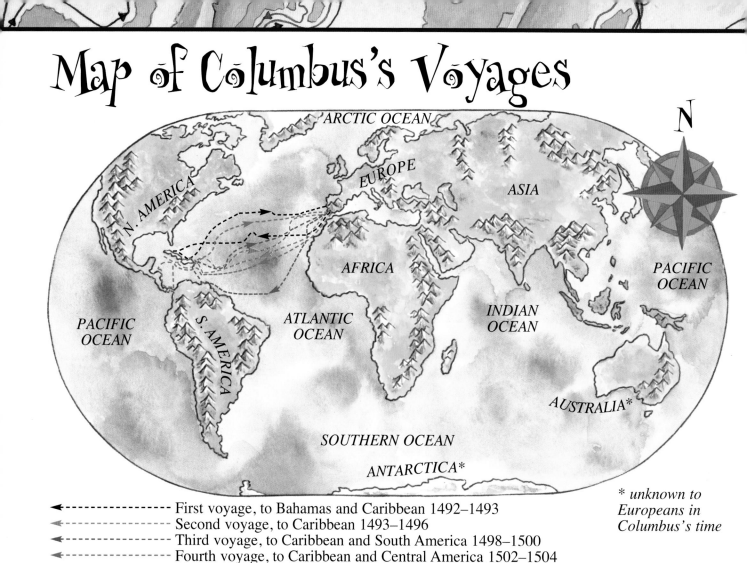

----◄-------------- First voyage, to Bahamas and Caribbean 1492–1493
----◄-------------- Second voyage, to Caribbean 1493–1496
----◄-------------- Third voyage, to Caribbean and South America 1498–1500
----◄-------------- Fourth voyage, to Caribbean and Central America 1502–1504

* unknown to Europeans in Columbus's time

After making his historic first voyage across the Atlantic, Columbus landed in the Bahamas (he thought they were Japan), Cuba (he thought it was China), and Haiti (the western part of the island of Hispaniola, sometimes known as Española). Columbus and his crew nearly died in a terrible storm on the voyage back to Spain, but Columbus was determined to return to the "fertile and beautiful" lands he had visited. To raise money for three more voyages, he claimed to have found "many spices and great mines of gold." He made plans to take control of the local Caribbean peoples, and make them work for European settlers as slaves.

Author:
Fiona Macdonald studied history at
Cambridge University and at the University of
East Anglia. She has taught adult education, and
in schools and universities, and is the author of
numerous books for children on historical topics.

Artist:
David Antram was born in Brighton, England,
in 1958. He studied at Eastbourne College of Art
and then worked in advertising for 15 years before
becoming a full-time artist. He has illustrated
many children's nonfiction books.

Series Creator:
David Salariya was born in Dundee, Scotland.
He has illustrated a wide range of books and has
created and designed many new series for
publishers both in the UK and overseas. In 1989 he
established The Salariya Book Company. He lives
in Brighton, England, with his wife, illustrator
Shirley Willis, and their son, Jonathan.

Editor:
Michael Ford

© The Salariya Book Company Ltd MMXIV
No part of this publication may be reproduced in whole or
in part, or stored in a retrieval system, or transmitted in any
form or by any means, electronic, mechanical, photocopying,
recording, or otherwise, without written permission of the
publisher. For information regarding permission, write to the
copyright holder.

Published in Great Britain in 2014 by
The Salariya Book Company Ltd
25 Marlborough Place, Brighton BN1 1UB
ISBN-13: 978-0-531-21177-9 (lib. bdg.)   978-0-531-22853-1 (pbk.)
All rights reserved.
Published in 2014 in the United States
by Franklin Watts
An imprint of Scholastic Inc.
Published simultaneously in Canada.

A CIP catalog record for this book is available
from the Library of Congress.

Printed and bound in Shanghai, China.
Printed on paper from sustainable sources.
Reprinted in MMXVII.
5 6 7 8 9 10 R 23 22 21 20 19 18 17

SCHOLASTIC, FRANKLIN WATTS, and associated logos are
trademarks and/or registered trademarks of Scholastic Inc.

This book is sold subject to the
conditions that it shall not, by way of trade or otherwise, be lent,
resold, hired out, or otherwise circulated without the publisher's
prior consent in any form or binding or cover other than that
in which it is published and without similar condition being
imposed on the subsequent purchaser.

PAPER FROM
SUSTAINABLE
FORESTS

You Wouldn't Want to Sail With Christopher Columbus!

...and this is the thanks I get!

Uncharted Waters You'd Rather Not Cross

Written by
Fiona Macdonald

Illustrated by
David Antram

Created and designed by
David Salariya

Franklin Watts®
An Imprint of Scholastic Inc.
NEW YORK • TORONTO • LONDON • AUCKLAND • SYDNEY
MEXICO CITY • NEW DELHI • HONG KONG
DANBURY, CONNECTICUT

Contents

Introduction

The year is A.D. 1492. The place is Palos, a harbor town in southwestern Spain. You are a bright young lad, but your parents are poor. Your father repairs boats and your mother sells shrimp in the marketplace. You're ten years old and it's time for you to find a job to help support your family. Some boys on your street are already working. They run errands and wash pots and pans at the inn. Others are training for skilled jobs as blacksmiths or carpenters. A few have joined the crews of fishing boats. You don't want to have jobs like these! Secretly, you dream of becoming an explorer and having amazing adventures in faraway lands. Who knows, one day you might have the chance to sail on a long ocean voyage. Before you board a ship, think carefully. Are you ready to leave your family, suffer months of hardship and danger, and possibly lose your life?

So You Want to Go to Sea

Spain borders the Mediterranean Sea and the wide Atlantic Ocean. It has busy harbors all around its coast. For centuries, Spanish people have relied on the sea to make a living. Many have become sailors and fishermen, but others have not left dry land. They've built ships, sewn cloth to make sails, hammered iron into anchors, twisted ropes, knotted nets, and crafted wooden chests and barrels. They've worked hard to unload ships' cargoes and built huge warehouses to store them. With all these different jobs on shore to choose from, are you sure that you still want to go to sea?

Why traveling by sea is best:

TRAVELING BY SEA has many advantages, especially over long distances or when carrying bulky cargoes. Making journeys over land (below) can be difficult and dangerous.

CROSSING RIVERS can be difficult. You'll find broken bridges and slippery stones.

IN SUMMER, you'll suffer from thirst, heatstroke, and exhaustion.

YOU'LL HAVE TO FIGHT off fierce bandits that wait to rob travelers.

IN WINTER, you'll face frostbite and sink up to your neck in snow.

MAKE SURE you don't fall off your horse, or into a pothole.

Why Do You Want to Explore?

You know that exploration is the latest craze among clever people and merchants seeking fortune. Ships from nearby Portugal have made voyages along the coast of Africa looking for a sea route to India. You've seen rich people wearing precious silks and jewels brought back from the Far East and you've smelled the rich Arabian perfumes they wear. There's a rumor in town that a stranger has arrived at the monastery to talk to monks and scholars there. His name is Christopher Columbus and he's planning a voyage.

Eastern treasures:

CUSTOMERS all over Europe will pay high prices for goods brought from Asia and the Middle East.

PEPPER

SILK

MEDICINES

SCENTS

GOLD AND PRECIOUS STONES

RIVALS! The kings of Spain and Portugal (above) both want to conquer lands in Asia and control the profitable trade in silks, jewels, and spices.

IMAGO MUNDI. Columbus used a book called *Imago Mundi*, or "Picture of the World," to support his ideas that the Atlantic could not be a wide ocean.

All explorers are fools! They'll fall off the edge of the world!

Iceland

ATLANTIC
OCEAN

Europe

Africa

Columbus so far:
1451 Born Genoa, Italy.
1465 Sails merchant ships in Mediterranean.
1476 Moves to Portugal, and makes plans for voyage to the East.
1484 Asks King John of Portugal for money. King John refuses.
1485 Moves to Spain.

Handy Hint

Remember, for centuries scholars have argued that the world is round, even though it looks flat!

RECENT EXPLORATION (above). In the past few years, explorers have already sailed northwest, beyond Iceland, and southwest, to remote islands in the Atlantic Ocean.

It says in *Imago Mundi* that the Earth is round.

Yes...and between the end of Spain and the beginning of India lies a narrow sea that can be sailed in just a few days.

9

How Would You Pay for the Voyage?

Approaching the rich:

MOST EXPLORERS need money to go on their expensive voyages. There are a few tricks you should know.

FLATTERY (above). Praise the queen's noble birth, generous nature, and reputation.

NATIONAL PRIDE (right). Tell the king that he'll win lasting fame for backing your voyage.

olumbus is making plans for an extraordinary adventure. He believes that he can reach Japan — the easternmost country known to Europeans — by sailing west across the Atlantic Ocean. Columbus doesn't have any money to pay for his voyage. Buying just one ship is extremely expensive and, for safety, he really needs two or three. Columbus must persuade rich people to help him. Over five years ago, in 1486, he asked the king and queen of Spain for money. They turned him down. Columbus never gave up hope and earlier this year (1492) he asked again. This time, he's lucky! Queen Isabella has said she'll pay for his voyage!

Turned down? You could:

INHERIT. If you're lucky, an elderly relative will leave you a fortune when he or she dies.

BE ENTERPRISING. Sell shares or persuade businessmen to invest in your voyage.

BE WARLIKE. Spend a year as a soldier and take prisoners. They'll pay large sums to be set free.

11

How Would You Prepare Your Fleet?

Food for the voyage:

BISCUITS are hard, tasteless, and full of weevils!

SALT OR PICKLED MEAT. Scrape the mold off before you eat it.

DRIED PEAS are either too hard or too mushy.

CHEESE is very smelly and full of worms.

FISH is caught fresh, but it looks very strange and may not be edible!

WINE AND WATER. At sea, wine easily turns to vinegar and stored water becomes very salty.

Shipmates:

ABOUT 90 SAILORS have agreed to serve as crew. There are also 2 captains, 3 masters, 3 pilots, 3 boatswains, 3 stewards, 3 caulkers (to mend leaks), and a doctor — plus some government officials, who may be spies.

How exciting! Columbus has chosen your town as the home base for his fleet. He arrived last night, carrying orders from the king and queen. The people of Palos must find ships for Columbus, equip them with a crew, food, and drink, and have them ready to sail within 10 weeks! The townspeople are not very happy about this. They believe that Columbus's voyage will end in disaster.

The language barrier:

MAKE SURE your interpreter speaks the right language. Columbus is taking an Arabic-speaker with him to the Caribbean!

The townspeople do not cooperate. However, one sea captain, Martin Alonso Pinzon, realizes that this voyage is his great opportunity to win fame and fortune. He takes charge, stocks the ships, and recruits a rough-and-ready crew — including you!

Don't let any women on board — they're thought to be unlucky!

13

Could You Handle a Sailing Ship?

Columbus's three ships:

SANTA MARIA. Designed to carry cargo, it's strong but slow, and hard to control when out on the open sea.

Santa Maria

Pinta

PINTA. A caravel (ship with a sleek, narrow hull) fitted with big square sails. It's the fastest of Columbus's three ships.

Niña

NIÑA. A small, light caravel, fitted with triangular sails. It rides the waves and should be easy to handle, even in storms.

Columbus is taking three ships on this voyage, the *Pinta*, the *Niña*, and the *Santa Maria*. Like all other vessels, they are made of wood and are powered by the wind trapped in their sails. Handling a sailing vessel is not an easy task. It takes strength and experience to raise and lower the heavy sails, and real courage to climb the tall rigging. If too many sails are hoisted, the masts might crack, or the whole ship might capsize. If there are too few sails, the ship cannot steer a safe course and will drift dangerously at the mercy of the sea.

Whoosh!

Handy Hint

Learn to sew! One day, your life may depend on being able to mend a sail.

LOOK OUT. Don't get caught out by calms, or your ship will drift aimlessly.

Be a safe sailor:

DON'T GET CAUGHT up in the ropes used to raise and lower the sails.

FIRM GRIP. Don't fall from the rigging that holds the masts in place.

TIE the sails down firmly or they'll flap in the wind and might rip and blow away.

HOLD ON TIGHT when you climb the mast to reef (shorten) the sails in a gale.

15

Which Way Would You Steer?

You head west, across the Atlantic Ocean. Columbus thinks there's land in that direction. Plants unknown in Europe have washed up on shores facing west. Columbus has read books which make him think that Japan is only about 2,734 miles (4,400 km) away, but it's 9,320 miles (15,000 km) further! He calculates that he should reach it quickly. Just in case he doesn't, he's decided to keep two logbooks. One for himself, to record the true course he's steering. The other shows a safer route, closer to land, to calm the fears of crew members like you.

To help you navigate:

AN HOURGLASS measures time and calculates how far you've traveled westward every day.

Hourglass

AN ASTROLABE is used to work out your latitude (distance north or south of the equator).

Astrolabe

LOGBOOK. Make a note of your ship's journey in a logbook at the end of each watch.

Logbook

THROW a line and weight to check the depth of the water.

LOOKOUT. Send someone up to the crow's nest to spot hazards.

A COMPASS is used to check the ship's course.

Traverse board

Compass

Dividers

DIVIDERS (metal pincers) measure precise distances on charts and maps.

TRAVERSE BOARD. The helmsman marks each change of course by sticking a peg into a board.

Could You Cope on Board?

The crew's duties:

Pumping bilgewater

Cleaning the deck

Mending sails

Checking ropes

Inspecting cargo

Mending leaks

Life at sea is tough. You have to keep the boat "shipshape," or neat and safe, but it's crowded, cold, damp, smelly, and infested with fleas. It leaks and has to be pumped out every day. There are no beds or chairs, except in Columbus's private cabin, so you have to sleep anywhere you find space. You can't get used to the system of watches — four hours on duty, then four hours rest — so you feel tired all the time. Some older sailors amuse themselves by gambling, arguing, and criticizing Columbus.

EATING. Forget table manners. The cook spreads food out on deck and sailors help themselves.

WASHING. You can wash in seawater. But there's no soap and sailors do not shave.

THE TOILET is just a wooden seat attached to the side of the ship. When the weather's bad, find a dark place in the hold.

ITCHY? Ask other sailors to help comb the lice from your hair.

UGH! The bilges are usually full of slimy, smelly water.

RATS. Most ships are infested with them.

OBEY ORDERS, or you'll feel this whip on your back.

Would You Lose Hope?

It has been over two months since you sailed away from Spain, and there's still no sight of Japan. The crew starts to grumble that Columbus has made a mistake in his calculations. You wonder if you are all doomed to die. Everyone on board has done his best to keep a lookout for land, but with no success. On October 10th, the crew of your ship, *Santa Maria*, organize a protest to confront Columbus. They say that the voyage west has gone on long enough and demand that he turn the ships around to go home. Columbus refuses, and the men are still unhappy. Will there be a mutiny soon?

Hopeful signs of land:

MIST AND CLOUD. This sometimes gathers above islands.

BIRDS flying overhead. Most don't go far out to sea.

SEAWEED. It often grows in shallow waters close to land.

SHELLFISH and other creatures that like to live on beaches.

BRANCHES that have fallen off seaside trees.

SMELLS of sweat and sewage mean that people are nearby.

A GLOW on the horizon might mean houses, lights, and fires.

Could You Survive on Shore?

Land at last! It's Friday, October 12th. For the first time in months, you are standing on solid ground. You've just scrambled ashore, along with Columbus and his bodyguard. He's already claimed these islands for Spain! Now he's marching toward some local men. They seem friendly, but very surprised. In the distance, you can see their village. It has tall, round houses, with grass roofs.

If this is Japan, why aren't people wearing silk robes? Where are the jewels you hoped to find and the palaces roofed in gold? You can see that Columbus is puzzled too. He's captured seven local men to guide his ships in search of treasure and spices. The natives call these islands "Bahama," not Japan!

This isn't what I had in mind.

What you'll find as you explore:

HAMMOCKS. Slung between trees, they make comfortable beds — if you keep still!

TOBACCO. Taino people on the nearby island of Cuba breathe its smoke. Ugh!

YAMS. These huge roots are very nourishing. But how do you cook them?

Handy Hint

Be like the Taino people — cover your face and body with paint to keep mosquitoes away.

Where do you think they've come from?

IGUANA. These green, meaty lizards are best roasted. Are you hungry enough to eat one?

PEPPERS AND CHILIES. Test your tastebuds with these favorite fiery flavorings.

MAIZE. You need strong teeth to enjoy a meal of these golden-yellow corn cobs.

23

Would You Get Home Safely?

You've spent two months exploring. Columbus has landed on two big islands. He's named them Cuba and Española. He's very excited because he has seen people wearing gold necklaces on Española. This convinces him that Japan can't be far away. Like many of his tired crew, you're feeling homesick and you've caught a nasty tropical disease. Captain Pinzon sails away in the *Pinta*, saying that he's going back to Spain. The next day is Christmas Day and you are looking forward to a special meal. Then disaster strikes! The *Santa Maria* runs aground and water pours in. You have to abandon ship!

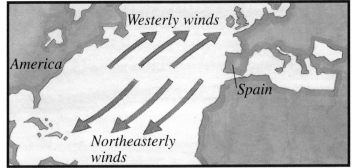

Northeasterly winds blew Columbus's ships from Spain toward America. He won't be able to sail back unless he heads north, where westerly winds blow.

Handy Hint

Make your voyage at the right time of year! Avoid the hurricanes that blow in spring and autumn.

What next?

LOAD as much as you can from the wreck of the *Santa Maria* onto the little ship *Niña* (left).

YOU DON'T have room for all the crew, so leave some men behind to build a settlement (right).

USE WOOD from the wreck to build a fort (left), to protect the men left behind from attack.

TAKE SOME TAINO people (right) back to Europe with you to show the king and queen.

SAY FAREWELL to the men left behind and set sail in the *Niña* (left).

SAIL as fast as you can! You don't want the *Pinta* to reach Spain before you and win all the glory!

25

Would You Make More Voyages?

THE SECOND VOYAGE. Columbus finds his first settlement destroyed by Tainos. He also hears that the local Carib people (below) are cannibals!

The *Niña* finally reached Palos harbor on March 15th, 1493. Soon after, Columbus received a hero's welcome from the king and queen, who eagerly agreed to pay for another voyage. They hoped he'd conquer more land, find more gold, and convert local people to Christianity. You sailed with Columbus on that second voyage, and on two more since then.

THE THIRD VOYAGE. Columbus makes slaves of the Tainos. The Spanish in the new settlement on Española rebel against him. Columbus gets very ill and is accused of fraud. He is sent home to Spain as a prisoner, in disgrace.

THE FOURTH VOYAGE. Columbus's ships are worm-eaten and his men are very weak. They are stranded on a sandbank in Panama, then marooned on Jamaica for a year.

But was this really a good idea? You've visited beautiful countries, but you've also seen a lot of death and disaster. Columbus fights with the local people and treats them like slaves.

Columbus's later voyages:

→ Second voyage (1493-1496)
→ Third voyage (1498-1500)
→ Fourth voyage (1502-1504)

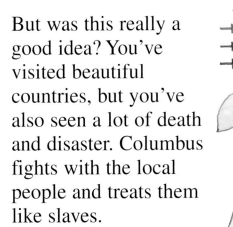

Cuba

Española

Jamaica

Central America

South America

Handy Hint

Pity the Carib and Taino people. Thousands die from diseases, such as the common cold, brought by Spanish settlers.

I wonder if I should have been a carpenter.

Would It All Be Worthwhile?

It's now 1504, and Columbus has made his last voyage. He's back home in Spain, tired, ill, bitter, angry, and deeply disappointed. His expeditions have exhausted him, but he's still as determined as ever. He spends his days trying to win back power and glory and still thinks that he reached the continent of Asia and the islands of Japan. He's sad and mistaken, but don't forget, his voyages changed our view of the world forever.

So, looking back at the time you spent with him and all the adventures you shared, do you think it was all worthwhile? If you were given the chance again, would you really want to sail with Christopher Columbus?

Columbus's final years:

1) ARCH ENEMY. The King of Spain appoints Columbus's rival, Nicolas Ovando, as governor of Española.

2) AMERICA is named after rival explorer, Italian Amerigo Vespucci, who sailed in 1499 and 1501.

3) RICH REWARDS? Columbus receives just one-fiftieth of the gold found on Española, not one-tenth as he hoped for.

4) COLUMBUS'S LETTERS to the Spanish king, begging forgiveness and favor, are thrown away.

5) DEATH. After Columbus dies in 1506, later explorers prove that many of his ideas were wrong.

6) COLUMBUS'S SON is made Admiral of the Ocean Sea and Governor of the Indies in his place.

Glossary

Astrolabe Metal disc with a pointer that helps sailors figure out their latitude.

Bilges The lowest part of a ship's hold.

Boatswain The shipboard manager.

Calms Dangerous weather at sea when the wind drops and ships drift with the tides.

Capsize To overturn.

Caravel A sailing ship with a sleek, narrow hull.

Carpenter Someone who makes things out of wood.

Caulkers Workers who mend leaks by filling gaps in ships' wooden hulls with old rope and tar.

Crow's nest The lookout post at the top of a ship's mast.

Dividers Metal pincers used for measuring distance on a map.

Enterprising Daring, energetic, and eager to make money.

Flattery Extravagant praise.

Frostbite Damage to the skin because of extreme cold.

Gale A strong wind.

Helmsman The man who steers a ship.

Hourglass A glass jar filled with sand that trickles slowly from top to bottom. It is used to measure time.

Hurricanes Violent storms.

Inherit Gain something from a relative when he or she dies.

Latitude Distance north or south of the equator.

Lead A heavy weight tied to a rope.

Marooned Left alone to starve on an island.

Master An expert sailor.

Monastery A place where monks live and work.

Mutiny A rebellion by soldiers or sailors.

Pothole A hole in a road.

Reef To shorten sails.

Rigging Ropes that hold a ship's masts in place.

Sea legs Experience of going to sea.

Ship's biscuit A hard, dry mixture of flour baked with water.

Shipshape Neat and safe.

Watch A period of duty on board ship.

Yams Tropical plants with swollen, fleshy roots.

Index

A New View of the World

Columbus sailed west because he wanted to make his fortune, and he knew that in Europe, Asian spices were worth more than gold. But he was also driven by a desire to find out more about the world beyond Europe.

Columbus was not alone in his thirst for knowledge. He lived during a time that historians now call the Renaissance. This period was at its height from around 1400 to 1600. At that time, scholars, writers, artists, scientists, and other thinkers rediscovered scientific theories and artistic styles surviving from ancient Greek and Roman times. They longed for new information and challenged accepted ideas.

As well as trying to confirm the ancient Greek theory that the world was round, Columbus and other early explorers also brought many "new" items from America to Europe.

These included pineapples, turkeys, spicy chilies, tomatoes, chocolate, and tobacco. Their voyages also led to European settlements in America and, later, to the transatlantic slave trade.

Columbus's voyage changed the world—and that is why we remember his bold, brave, dangerous, determined adventure to this day.

Some Other Top Explorers

Columbus's voyages inspired many other explorers to venture into the unknown. Here are just a few:

Ferdinand Magellan (Portuguese, 1470–1521) and **Juan Sebastián Elcano** (Spanish, 1476–1526) sailed from Spain in 1519 in search of Asian spices. They crossed the Atlantic, steered through the narrow strait at the southern tip of South America (now called the Strait of Magellan), and then crossed the Pacific. Magellan was killed in the Philippines, and many crewmen died of disease. Elcano sailed on with a few survivors. They crossed the Indian Ocean, sailed around Africa, and headed north, finally reaching home in 1522. They were the first people to sail around the world.

John Cabot (Italian, ca. 1450–ca. 1499) sailed from England in 1497 and crossed the North Atlantic. He landed in Newfoundland (now part of Canada), and was amazed by icy waters teeming with huge fish. In 1498 Cabot made a second voyage, hoping to engage in trade. No one is sure what happened, but he and many of his ships never returned.

Amerigo Vespucci (Italian, 1454–1512) crossed the Atlantic and sailed south, exploring the territory now known as Brazil in 1501–1502 and 1503–1504. He was the first to realize that the landmass he saw was not Asia, but a whole "New World," unknown to Europeans. Later, mapmakers named America after him.

Vasco Núñez Balboa (Spanish, ca. 1475–1519) founded the first permanent European settlement in the mainland Americas in 1510. Named Santa María, it was in present-day Panama. In 1513 Balboa was the first European to see the Pacific from the Americas.

Did You Know?

• Exploring was a deadly business. Magellan and Elcano set sail with around 237 crewmen. Four years later, only 18 men were still alive.

• Díaz de Solís is thought to have been eaten in a South American cannibal ceremony.

• Ponce de León spent years looking for the mythical Fountain of Youth. Its magic waters were said to make people live forever. Needless to say, he never found it.

• The kings of Spain and Portugal paid for many early explorers' voyages. In 1494 they agreed to divide the whole vast New World and all its treasures between them. No other Europeans were allowed a share—and no consideration was given to the Native American peoples who had been there first.

Juan Ponce de León (Spanish, 1474–1521), Governor of Puerto Rico, explored the coast of Florida in 1513.

Juan Díaz de Solís (Spanish, 1470–1516) sailed south in 1515 to the land now known as Uruguay, and began exploring the mighty River Plate. But soon after, he and most of his men were captured and killed by local people.

Giovanni da Verrazzano (Italian, 1485–1528) explored the North American coast, including the Hudson River and the land where the city of New York now stands.